IN IT

IN IT

Stephen Berg

University of Illinois Press

URBANA AND CHICAGO

PS
3552
.E7
.I5
1986

Publication of this work was supported in part by grants
from the National Endowment for the Arts and the Illinois
Arts Council, a state agency.

This book is printed on acid-free paper.

Library of Congress Cataloging-in-Publication Data
Berg, Stephen.
In it : poems.
I. Title.
PS3552.E715   1986   811'.54   85–28842
ISBN 0-252-01235-6 *(alk. paper)*

ACKNOWLEDGMENTS

Antaeus 47 (Autumn 1982): "The Rocks"
Antaeus 40–41 (Winter-Spring 1981): "Gratitude," "In It," "And the Scream"
Antaeus 30–31 (Summer-Autumn 1978): "A God," "In Our Life"
Iowa Review 13 (Winter 1982): "Three Voices"
Poetry, October 1985: "From the Bridge," "Nights after Reading"
Antioch Review, January 1986: "Now and Then," "One,"
"The Visit," "Big Mood"
Carla Weinberg helped me with my free version of Leopardi's
L'infinito. I also used Rexroth's and Lowell's versions.
My gratitude to Larry Lieberman
for his great care as my editor.
In It took final shape during the late winter and spring of 1984–85
while I was on a grant from The Dietrich Foundation. My thanks to
Dan and Jennie Dietrich for their generosity.

Cover lithograph: Sidney Goodman
Design: Cynthia Krupat

To my friends

—Charlie, Jeff, Michael—

hard to imagine the life or the work

without them.

Contents

IN IT

Leaves

More and more often as the years accumulate,
the life you are living inside you rises until it *is* you.
The moon, that ruined badge of lovers,
looks beautiful again, rueful, large;
the vacant street, dotted with garbage,
seems to be lighted differently, from within,
and death—*it happens, it can't but it will, when?*
to you—is only a fact you don't need explained.
It begins one night usually: one, then another.
Behind trees, leaves bickering between houses,
people drift in their rooms.
One works at a sink, one reads, one
sweeps, one faces you, his anonymous head very still,
you step to the window, stay, try to let him know
you know he's fixed across the way
watching you, daydreaming, waiting—for what?
Night is a pool of heat filling your breast,
a bearable, steady fear throbbing with images
that makes your nipples rise and will not cool.
Maybe you accept what seeps into you
to become you, deepening into itself.
Maybe the unconsoling stars, vapid, white,
like the eyes of massive, unnamed animals,
those black leaves struggling on a wall,
know. But a mindless voice
that has its passion, has its hunger, keeps
thrusting like an extra heart,
grows more like the actual touch
of hands and lips,

grows closer to the one you feel is you,
is you, is you, here,
in the flesh, *your* flesh, now.

The Rocks

The cold is here. Impossible to wake
those browns, greens, streaks of purple and gray
with spray from the hose, its nozzle plugged with ice,
impossible to enjoy
those faces, tangled in lily stalks and weeds.
One summer Sunday, wearing old sneakers,
Bill and I drove to the Wissahickon
and slid down the embankment to the creek,
soaking our pants as we knelt to pick out good ones,
rolling, lifting, cradling, cursing
as we kicked steps up the steep mushy sides
and stumbled out
and dropped them in the trunk,
then after five or six trips planted them here.
I loved kneeling on them stiff-armed with all my weight,
snugging them tighter into the dirt,
hearing the gritty shifting until each one fit.
Their muddy, unashamed aloneness,
their permanent, homely sorrow soothed me.
My favorite is right out of Buson's six-panel screen:
fierce, haggard, recklessly free, floating in air
or earthless, simply there,
a few touching, merging, all thirteen
brushed in a kind of accidental
poise without meaning or purpose.
The sketchy translucent strokes seem to tremble—
you can see through them—as if our fear of time, death,
        how
temporary we are is what the rocks are.
He lay the screen on the floor.

Just above it was a window clouds would glide across.
He'd look up at the clouds, then paint. Look up. Paint.
Drink wine late afternoons, watching the sun slip away.
Spend some days only leaning over it,
scouring its five-by-eleven whiteness,
unfocusing, lost in it, imagining
shapes live, shapes die,
flicking the dry bristles unconsciously with his thumb, not
    knowing
when, where—four months from his death—
the next rock would appear, bending abruptly,
filling, wielding his short-handled brushes faster and faster
    until
the ink ran out. Snow now,
gentle, wispy, far-apart, helpless flakes
the tiniest breeze gusts back up or shoots across,
then calm, and then they float straight down
slow, very slow. How good it seems,
exactly like late spring afternoons picnicking by the river—
long after people had finished eating,
wife, daughters, friends stretched on the grass talking,
forks, spoons, leftovers packed away—I'd stand, and,
    looking
beyond heads across the water, shake out our tablecloth
again again again
until my arms hurt and I couldn't hear,
then fold it into a white square,
drop it on the lidded wicker basket.

Day end. Blue wisps of light skimming the treetops. I
    remember thinking
trees, grass—their silence—that's probably why
we go to them, touch them, stare
as I did by the river—
unattached phrases, rhymes, half called-out images, "of
    time, death, how"
happening in my mind like whipcracks—
then at dusk I turned and lay with my family,
grass damp and cool,
geese massed for bread along the banks,
everything in shadow, shadow everywhere.

Visiting the Stone

Last week on my way to the shrink between connections
the drunk who's always sprawled on the El stop steps—
emaciated fingers, rags, bruised stumps—
pointed to his ankles where his feet should be
and shook a paper cup. I popped in a quarter,
stepped over his legs,
then caught the bus to my appointment.
For years I've been asking "Why?" "How?"
unraveling this story and that,
but what can explanation or advice do
when the answers don't apply?
This afternoon for the first time since they
set the stone ten years ago, unpolished gray Vermont
    granite
embellished with a three-inch etched border
of bare vines, I knelt at my father's grave,
memorizing his dates chiseled in the marker,
and asked him, too,
then brushed off clusters of dried pine needles, dirt-streaks,
in the field of dwarfish stones. *You*
his voice flashed like a scar on air
its cold, useless answer.

To Charlie

A broom, its straws bleached, tips bent, leans
against a green plastic hose coiled
on the side of the house above the drain,
every few seconds one
slow long drop slips from the nozzle,
yellow, orange, and blue lilies stick out between
rocks Bill and I hauled from the Wissahickon
at least five years ago. Now
we're fifty, now in a letter from Charlie—
"One can get terribly frightened of age, aging."
What was it yesterday that made me so happy?
For one instant—no
people, street, sky, ominous glass buildings—
I stood there, not a thought or question,
no trace of the inevitable "Why?"
that loves giving its bitterness to me.

No Word

Inside each of us
there's a mammoth dome of light
like the one sheltering me
when I walked out that night
alone in the middle of pines
in Maine, near the ocean.
Black wherever I looked,
even my arms and hands.
I reached out and grabbed a spray of needles,
then tried to see down the path
I knew went in front of me
through elms and brush to water.
Nothing. So I looked up
and found it, flowing in its white fires above my face,
with no word for what it is,
as when a face turns toward you
on the street and you recognize
someone you do not know.

Nights after Reading

Sometimes, dozing for hours,
books open on the couch, hearing
descriptions of death, partings, the sea,
humanity learning to love itself
too late, I think I even hear
pieces of me in the characters roaming those pages—
Levin, for one, or that dumb, righteous government
        official
dying of cancer who discovers life with only days left
after he breaks through the "black sack"
and light transfigures every cell of his miserable existence.
Tolstoi, is Ivan Illych us, was he you, are we
all doomed never to comprehend our lives?
In your *Last Diaries*
you attack the horror of death, attack the "I"
because you can't believe you'll die,
you must prove we have "souls."
I touch the cool gray pages.

Both

It's almost a month since we touched, or wanted to,
that's why I bought these dense, yellow-headed flowers.
All the way home
I kept putting my nose to the chopped stem-ends
that soaked in the grocer's pail and held the scent of earth.
Dry now after a week, still bright on our kitchen table,
they fan out of the vase I stuck them in.
Each day a few petals drop to the varnished wood.

Monet's *Cloud, 1903,* is nearly all water
but at the top a narrow chunk of the pond's bank
is a sky of shaggy weeds.
Upside down in the water two clouds float:
one's crisp, tight; one's fuzzy, larger.
Lemon and pink lilies glow on their pads,
sitting in the life I envy;
at the bottom two white ones jut out,
taller than the others, surrounded by heavy leaves.

Some nights, trying to kill what haunts us, what is us,
we scream at each other until we can't speak.
Our skin can't bear the touch of the other's hand.
We sleep on the edges of our bed.
The clouds in the middle of the water, going nowhere,
don't know what's happening to us either.

What is happening?
A full moon eases across our window.
We stare at each other across the table
who have lived together so many years
hearing the vein-blue echoings of self-in-the-other

flushed by the terrified, helpless child within
until it shows itself when we stand close,
clear as the thin oil and tiny hair
of each pore of our faces.

Two blue-white strokes rush through the painting and stay
    there,
raised slashes of anger, scars, troubling the scene.

The twine you tied from the rusted iron socket outside
the kitchen window to the drainpipe has broken.
The vines you planted months ago have pulled it down.
They lie woven in each other at our feet, flame-blue
morning glories pointing in all directions,
slim yellow throats and dusty tongues
silent, gaping with hunger.

Trash trapped under tires, envelopes ripped across one
    edge,
newspapers flapping on a fallen beam, sky
through the glassless windows of a shell,
a mattress, its black intestinal springs and poor, coarse hair
    drooling
from a gash, stray green weeds poked through, the intact
    parts of its ticking pooled with stains—

the back door open behind us, we stand side by side
    absolutely still, knuckles so close their warmth
    touches,
the moon, stalled across from the sun at this hour, dawn, a
    translucent, pitted eye.

Last Elegy

Surgeons cutting a hole
in my father's skull
with one of those saws that lift
a plug out of bone also took
a big lump off my spine
in the dream I don't understand
that flickered back
the day before he died.
We were at the shore following
a golf match on TV,
eating, napping. His drained
gray face didn't reveal
any sense of being here,
any desire to live.
The money he made,
the failure he thought he was
in love, in business,
intensified his mood
after the heart attack.
The sky blew flat, smeary gray,
a few fly-like figures
paced the cold beach. Millie,
Clair, Margot, Mom and I
didn't know how to stop his
staring out of nothing into nothing,
so we watched hard
Nicklaus miss two easy putts
and other famous pros tee off
with that quick fluid swing
they have, then stroll down

the fairway to the ball,
the whole world manicured, green.

To say "I love you"
meant "I know I'm dying,"
but you said it,
at least I think I heard you
whisper it to me. Or was it to yourself?
I kept my eyes on the screen.

Three Voices

[*For Charlie*]

1

Late one night—one of those mild, hazy nights
just before Christmas—elated, buzzing with wine,
I dialed the house you were renting on Laguna Beach.
No answer. I imagined you
gazing until it got light—
phosphorescent whitecaps skittering through darkness,
faint lines of code loaded with meaning,
dissolving at your feet.

I needed talk about poetry, women, one of those talks
when we say anything to find
insight, truth—lost instantly: you feel it, see it, can't say
      what it is—
its doomed, wordless afterimage stabbing the air.
We've no identity then,
we're anyone, anything—faces, walls,
windows vacant and stark, words on a page,
is, is quavering in every cell.

I sat in my kitchen with the lights off,
hearing Giacometti's despair—
in his *Notebooks* he writes he couldn't sculpt a head
the way he saw it, "the way it is,"
but it wasn't only that.
He couldn't believe consciousness includes death, *his*
      death:
"He goes on speaking, but he's dead . . . is he dead?"

16

seeing himself awake at the moment of death,
suffering what James warns in his story
about the fear of love becomes "the horror of waking."

A skinny, agonized, bent, bronze arm perched on a steel
    rod,
its hand splayed, is Giacometti's scream,
corkscrewing up through your chest into your throat and
    out
when no one else is there—
the aloneness of life,
how strange and miraculous it is,
how it simply is, how all is.

Tonight is another night like that.
This desk, this lamp, this paper, these too familiar hands.
In a cone of light below me
a man in a loose, brown, buttonless overcoat
hacks with a handax a sawed-off chunk of branch pinned
    under his foot,
making short pieces, splinters, stacking them against a wall
of the shack he sleeps in in somebody's yard.
Each time he slashes the ax down breath
puffs from his lips the way words bud, blossom
between us and immediately die. . . .

2

"Do you ever think about yourself?"
A kind, unindulgent shrink I knew

answers, "Almost never. . . ."
In Princeton, years later,
a teacher from Japan, a short man dressed in a shiny gray
    suit,
asks, after I tell him I'm in pain,
"Who is the I?"
twists his right hand like a corkscrew
above his head and says, "This is the sharpest sword in the
    world—
it can cut anything—can it cut itself?"
"No. No. No. Be the sword!" I blurt out.
Sitting next to me in the stuffy third-floor office,
my friend Jeff growls, "Of course it can!" Adamant, sure.
"The ego has no foundation, you know . . ." the teacher
    says.
I stand: "I'm standing here—on the *floor!*"
"Show me where you're standing," he says.
I hesitate, look down, step back, and point to where I *was*
and we start laughing. "Why didn't you do *this?*" I hear,
and he walks toward me, stops, his breath warm on my
    face,
his eyes my eyes, my eyes his, for
one split second nothing mine.

3

This morning, waiting for the 33
a block from the halfway house near my house:
one of those old, moronic baby-men
who lounge in the sun on a bench all day

or scrounge candy wrappers, pennies, butts, then ring
your doorbell for a quarter, skips up to me,
leans on me, tilts his head, smiles up at me
and I ask Do you ever take the bus? *No No* he utters,
shaking his head, *No! No!* Do you ever go downtown? *Oh*
    No No No
he answers, urgent, sure. *Can't even find my mother*
he confesses, solemnly. How old are you? *Sixteen.* . . .
His toothless, wizened bag of a face, adolescently shy,
points down at the pavement to avoid me, to escape being
    seen,
as the bus comes and the doors fold open
and I hop up and in, on the reeling floor,
squeezed between a fat black lady clutching a Bible,
hugging a pole with her free arm, and a man with a curly,
    stiff red beard
who flashes his age card at the driver.
Poor sweet little guy—shod in white socks, blue plastic
    shower shoes
squashed at the heels—he shuffles back
to his brothers and sisters, stops, turns, waves at me
following him through the bus window as we pull away
No No Oh No No No No No

After a Death

The people you told your pain to
are shaking their fists at you,
calling you the most selfish, cruel person
they ever knew because they heard
themselves, not only your crazy fear-stunned voice
groping for someone to save you,
to hold you back from death. You'll echo
in them forever, they think, they think
you'll tip them into hell
or death, and maybe you will,
but that happens, so why not say that too
and not apologize or explain,
why not tell them what it was to be you
trying to leave crumbs of yourself
in a few friendly hands.

The Visit

At the clear heart of the paperweight in green,
carved, pastel ice
where you'd expect a village snow scene
whose flakes twirl and fall when you shake it
is *Don't Forget Your Mother!*
Nothing moves. The message floats there,
a heart-shaped fan opens behind it,
cheap greeting-card pink. Thin as hair
a few black abstract flourishes
as if scratched by a nervous fingernail
hang here and there like Heidegger's "thought paths."
It used to be in the city, now it sits
on a teak end table by a window
in my mother's condo at the shore,
clouds, roofs, unrecognizable domestic things,
the sea, glittering in it.
Right now she cleans,
dusting knickknacks and shelves. I watch from a chair.
Sweet whiffs of bacon, toast, eggs, coffee. "Reaaady!"
Mouth open, too, at twenty,
arms raised in terror or surprise,
on the table
in an oval silver frame
up to my waist in surf, in black and white, I
yell toward some lost face on the beach
whose unrelenting timeless absence echoes.

Insomnia

I slip out of bed and take a piss
and go off into one of our rooms to think, to be alone.
Portraits and snapshots fill the mantel, give the walls
finite existence—
women who lived to ninety, kids on the beach, kids
nuzzling a parent's leg, faked smiles at graduation,
cousins, days in Maine, so much done
for its own dear sake at the time,
as if only what *has* happened to and with us
exists, and time's that.
Before I know it it's five.
The dog asleep on the kitchen floor downstairs
grunts, lets out two heavy sighs,
the first birds start their long, awkward tirade.
Color and black and white
book titles, ashtrays, lamps, who is where when
like darkroom images in developer emerge.
Men at this age know nothing, words less and less console.
I tiptoe back to bed and curl next to
the sleeping life that breathes as it has next to me
for twenty-five years, and knows, I need to believe,
some absolute truth that can save me,
and mumbles: "I need to tell you something—
it's like there's a kind of bitter, heavy thing
pulling down my chest inside, my mouth,
my whole life . . . can I say *any*thing to you?"
Three hours later, backs to each other,
our feet touch the floor;
we sit on each side of the bed,

etched in white light,
consigned to this place as in Dante's
eternal Now
where the soles of sinners' feet
are pure fire.

And the Scream

The thirtyish, Irish, red-nosed carpenter
who works for Coonan—he rehabs houses up here—
is already half stoned on beer
before eight and chases his son past my front window,
screaming at him, the kid's glasses,
thick as my little finger,
bobbling on his nose.
Thin steady pewter drizzle,
long smudges yellowing the sky,
clouds darkening the street abruptly,
Pat and Jack Laurent's house gloomy
across from mine (they're away), even the embroidery
of lace curtains, the high-
arched Victorian double doors
incapable of lightening the mood.
That boy disappearing between houses
reminds me of when I
punched my whole arm through the glass door
between our dining room and kitchen
(the maid wouldn't leave it open)
and gashed my elbow so it bled on the floor
big splashes and wouldn't stop
and my mother's or the maid's or my
scream seemed to echo everywhere. That boy—
from my living room one night, in the dark,
I watched his father screaming, waving a beer bottle
above the mother stretched out in a slip in bed under
a hatless four-bulb ceiling fixture's neutral blue-white
        glare.
Nobody would call this poetry.

When I leaf through serious books, though, I see
blindings, suicides, revelations,
some lust that breeds disaster.
Families and blood are what we want—
because we need love or can't love?
For example, my mother tells me (we're face-to-face in her
      living room,
she will not look at me when she speaks)
her mother had to pick lice from her scalp when she was
      ten,
her piano-prodigy Christian Scientist brother
refused help from a doctor so he died at twenty-six,
coughing blood into a bucket while she watched. Poor.
      Crazy.
And so on, and so on, and therefore—
incomplete sentences, true,
sketches merely,
like watching a scream through glass, as I have twice
      lately,
filling in the detail of hearing
plus all the other crap: motives, stupidities,
money, sex, "the real reason," someone always dying.
But what I need to say is—
Yes, merely a sketch, that's it,
that's us, half-known, unredeemable animals,
and the scream, the scream.

Riding Back

After the party to raise money
we waited at the bus stop for the 33,
jigged in the raw wind, hugging each other,
kissing and joking.
We were in love that moment, free of everything,
even our kids. I started screaming
nutty, meaningless things I can't remember
and cupped your ass and kissed your tits through the tweed
        coat,
pulled you against me, my back to a fierce gust.
Three blocks from us
the filthy, restless Delaware slid through the city, the bus
braked, wheezed, its blank windows glared florescent blue,
its doors flipped apart.
You spilled change into the box, we took a seat,
still laughing, playing with each other
as it jolted off—us and the driver.
Oh the silence of that trip home then
past everything familiar—
the Hospital Supplies' chrome and pink limbs and trusses,
the Chestnut Street Arcade, the silly
adult game and toy store,
the pure linen blouses on mannequins in Bonwit's
        windows,
the flats, the shorts cut full, military,
flared at the crotch for the sweet cruise to nowhere.

On a Page

Indecipherable, huge words are
scrawled in the corners of the torn fan paper
where Hiroshige's scorpion fish lie on each other,
mouths open, gasping, endlessly hungry
for the green sea scallion
they love. Their blood-colored fins and tails
flash and look as though they could cut
like the grief that still slashes me when I can face it.
They drift on the blue floor, nudging each other
amid stems of ginger.
One with creamy spots all over, head pointing down,
mouth angrily groping,
reminds me of myself, of the stupidity and pain
that start late some nights. The other one waits.

In Blue Light

Stealing a dollar once just before dawn
from my father's thick wallet on the dresser
while he slept, I saw how innocent he was
facing the ceiling, not seeing anything.
Four or five feet away my mother lay on her side.
Tie clip, key ring, loose change
shifted while I teased it out
and watched his things grow clearer in blue light:
Trojans, their foil packets glinting,
business cards, the hanky from his jacket pocket
still folded, clean, white. Why was I there?
His eyes twitched, relaxed, he snorted
once, twice, three, with the last inch of the money—
clinkings, breaths—. I was twelve.
Minutes later, waiting in the bright street, I thought
back to their bodies, to the boy-ghost hovering there, and
fist in my pocket, crushed the bill,
then pulled it out and let the gutter have it.

The Voice

Older girls taunted me into one of those
apartment-house basement window wells;
I crouched in that waist-high hole,
hoping they'd go away. Like a bunch of birds
pecking at crumbs they'd flirt and try to kiss me.
After they'd had their fun I'd talk to myself down there,
my Dad's flat, gravely voice was mine,
a twin, bodiless soul
echoing against moist cement walls.
There are quaint streaks of noise inside my head
that are him talking, sometimes cursing the beautiful
mistake of life, sometimes asking how I am—
memory, I guess, but who knows, maybe
it's really him, yearning because he's lonely,
my grouchy old man asking me to a movie,
how the children are, about money,
"How's the poetry business?"—maybe
it is the rich ash of his bones and flesh
learning to speak again.

Late Spring

Sitting up ahead of me on someone's doorstep,
a fat woman in a housedress stamped with faded purple
blotches of flowers juts her legs apart,
the thigh closest to me

blocking the other leg, her skirt hiding the near leg down
      to the ankle,
angled across her lap to the hip, apparently accidental
—like those times at a play
waiting for it to begin when you watch the middle

of the curtain where it isn't quite closed and catch
flashes of hands, secret preparations through the black
      crack.
I'm half a block away. Then I'm in front of her and look.
No underpants, no awareness on her face—of her, of
      me—

no change of her large, wet, doll eyes,
and I can gaze directly at it:
delicately hairy, bearded, Mandarin-like, innocent,
the lips that could have been unbearable to see

not there—thank God, not in sight.
In Logan Square halfway to the center of town
child-sized copper frogs squirt water, three giant
nude female and male bronze gods, in the immune, aloof
      postures of sheer pleasure,

relax beneath sheets of water gushing from nozzles behind
   their heads.
Stripped tulips circle the pool, nothing but stalks;
a few stray bits of paper, cellophane;
sprawled, rain-flattened leaves, clipped hedges;

weeds up in ragged clumps; a chaos of red petals
stuck to the dirt and grass.
Her casual, idiot presence made it all ordinary,
she oozed indifference like a goddess, like this May
   morning,

the glistening frogs and gods joyous in a heaven of static,
   self-contained passion,
whiffs of old age blowing from houses, potatoes boiling,
the irises (that's what they were) adrift on her sleazy rayon
   frock,
replicas of death.

Remembering Leopardi's Moon

A VERSION

Moon, the year is over.
I scaled this hill a year ago to see you.
My heart was rapid and cold, you
floated over the maples, over there,
the same pasty communion wafer you are now,
you made each leaf visible,
you made the road leaving this fortress glow like an eerie
    snake.
But I could barely see. I stood there, crying.
In a dream, on one of those nights
when I know I'll die, the whole world
looked crippled, poor, free, everyone stood outside
pointing at you, whispering.
Moon, if I love anyone, it is you.
And then I love a girl fondling me, and games, and my
    body
when it was straight, gray-veined, milky,
before my father's violence turned it ugly.
It feels good to look back,
to count how many years I've lived,
to resurrect images of childhood. Time—
death, love—quivered with hope then.
I'd climb trees and let myself slip from the top,
trusting the branches to break my fall.
You'd be there, guarding me.
But I feared violent noises and the dark.
At ten, my life was over.
I'd sit in my father's stone library
and read, read with my brother Carlo

in an alcove, drop off to sleep in his lap,
reading. I was healthy until I was ten.
From ten to seventeen I sat in that jail and read—
my father forced me—
until I became those pages: yellow, infinite.
But I won't waste time now trying to see again
what was. Pain's made the world abstract.
Clouds, stars, the night: that's all. Moon,
where are you? Look at me: a hunchback
dressed like a stupid, vicious priest. Pure black.
I pit language against despair each minute of each day
to breathe, to act, not to feel crazy—
the only way I can touch you.

Nothing exists, not even this voice of mine,
these simple words. Illusions are gone:
desire, hope, these two
that made waking possible, dawn after dawn.
They used to make me tremble,
but nothing has value, earth does not care,
life is the narrowness of this poem,
the grind of composition, and what I write—
truculent, useless (though it begs to live)—
is dust even before it reaches your ears.
Sleep. Go back to the chaos of beginnings. Stay there.
No moon above those cool, featureless trees: black
emptiness, which is time, which is—
if we can bear it—all the world is.
The mute path of the stars is crazed, magnificent.
The breeze just now freshens my heavy face.

33

Nature, sickness, people struggling to love—
what do they mean? Time is the breath of gods,
the air of cities and rich fields,
it gorges each thought, cell, blood and bone,
it is the gods, it is our consciousness,
it means we now
are,
we are,
you, I,
(oh why isn't a hand rubbing my twisted spine?)
are,
each word next to a word stone.

Infinity

That hill out there—I've always loved it!—
and this hedge, cutting in front of me,
blocking the horizon, the last step to infinity.
Sitting here, stunned by a dream of space
beyond all hills and hedges, I hear
silence erasing man's possibilities.
A calm starts inside me and stays for awhile.
Wind roughing the trees, weighed against silence, is
    eternity.
This is the season of the mind—
the dizzying gulf of sky, the abyss of self—
one distant, visible; one close as my own skin—
each impossible to know or to touch,
this is the time when consciousness and thought and I
are nameless, nothing, not here. I love it—
the one true freedom: letting my mind sink
like a ship in mid-ocean whose keel
is gashed by some invisible
fist and goes down with the sweet ease of a rock.

Down

A VERSION OF ARCHILOCHUS

Wait. Listen. Don't move.
There's a girl working in your house
who's so beautiful, so alive
anyone would want her.
We should sit down
some evening over wine and I'll tell you
how often I've seen in my mind
the tight silky hair of her cunt
glistening beneath the moon
and wanted to ease my tongue in.
Remember that great saying—
Love gives men things other than the pure face of God to enjoy—?
I confess
once, months ago,
I took her into the fields—it was spring: shaggy
tall red flowers bobbed in the grass everywhere.
I helped her down and slid my hands under her neck
and pillowed her with my wool cloak.
She sat up for a second, afraid,
but I kissed her nipples gently, with such tenderness
how could I stop myself
from dropping between her thighs.
She quieted and let me touch her everywhere,
her firm skin shone, sweating with lust,
I licked her throat, armpits, feet, navel, knees,
and in her for the first time came
the moment my wild cock
sank halfway in-
to her thick, blond, flowery bush.

36

On the Day of Atonement

There's God!
Newspapers rolled up, crammed in his jacket pockets,
hunched over, crossing,
recrossing the street, talking to houses,
cracked glasses, bleary eyes, fat,
socks peeled down, in sandals, yelling
"Don't fall over, whatever you do!"

God has nobody anymore and walks around in rags,
stuttering, insulting people, thinking
"Everyone's stronger than me," thinking "They know, They
    know. . . ."

It's so lovely
not to see earth anymore,
only holy visions,
never wash, sleep on benches, once a year
get quick fifty-cent Bowery haircuts done with clippers,
scalp streaks glaring through black filthy hair.

In Our Life

Snow fallen overnight, not heavily.
It shines on the thickest branches and on the street
where ruts and footprints break through.
A floppy, purplish leaf, old portraits
of the women in your family, battered silver spoons—
signs of you everywhere,
so much tenderness for you
I forget where I am.
Jars filled with seeds flatten in the drizzly light
on a windowsill, a bowl
stacked with seashells on a table seems too small,
and knowing you will die someday shudders through me.
I dreamt
you were a stick of chalk,
you couldn't move or speak
when I leaned over and held
and kissed your face and shook you—
in the same dream last night
a woman walked day after day without knowing why
and called my name without knowing why,
wounded by the newspapers and the city
and the blade of her own mind that split her mind.
I woke, knowing I'm her, as you are,
half our lives gone, listening to the house
speak through its cool brick and timber. The furnace starts,
the ducts creak, I climb
to my third-floor room. No pears yet
on the tree. A sparrow, in the first warmth,
spurts from branch to branch, free. Pain, like its

indelicate blunt head, jabs
and waits. Its beak opens,
sometimes to sing.

Summer Twilight

Sitting here,
doing nothing,
I let my open hands
find the warm stone step
the way I'd touch a woman
for the first time,
I look up and see
the street lamps flare,
men drifting to their stoops
to finish a drink,
bask in the peaceful weather,
small figures in calm air.
On a smooth white wall
I think I see
a shadow judging me,
shaky, familiar, thin,
that can show up anywhere
any time it decides,
its weightless life
like the silence in a room
after lovers
have talked, made love, talked again
and, shorn of purpose,
drifted off to sleep.
In an earlier place
the boy I think I was
would stay out late
waiting for the ice truck—
no one really exists
no one's to blame

running through his mind—
then when it parked for deliveries
he'd scoop loose daggers
off the tailgate, stand there
chewing until his teeth hurt.

Little Mood

When it rains
I know what death is
as it sweeps through branches,
glazing the trunks.
People sit with each other,
nothing to say,
bearing the uselessness of things,
a fog clings to sewers, grass,
love is an eye
as blank as what it sees,
blanker than the blank sky.

Big Mood

The people who came here first
from Puerto Rico's calm, crisp air,
their lighted plastic Christs and tin window decorations—
roses, Virgins, scenes of the Nativity—
gutted, half-rehabed, finished shells,
the gleam of fresh paint on a door,
on a sunny day this
"It is enough to be here
I accept things as they are"
makes being a man
miraculous, sane,
makes the plain act of standing here
on my front steps
considering loose bricks tamped lengthwise
into the dirt bordering our bent young cherry
complete, like being what I see, like air.

Sad Invective

The man who sold his business to a business is looking for
    a business.
I went to high school with him, we played ball, he was a
    great second base.
Let's say he made eight million on the deal, selling his
    Dad's Brixite factory—that's what I heard—
and can't find anything exciting to do. Let's say he's used
    up pleasure.
What happens when you reach the end of money, is it like
    being sent to bed, age three, before you got tired?
You'd lie up there in the lonely dark, listening to the
    grown-ups,
trying to pick up from their dull static of words
your name, stories about the real world.
Do you ever feel the way I do: wanting money after
    fucking, money
before eating, money in handmade envelopes under the
    bed, money
stitched to your thighs, money that can't run out?
Man's first cure for the poison of error was money.
Having a lot of money means everyone loves you, you
    can't die.
And pain is beautiful when you're rich.
And even being sick is fun. Let's consider this a religious
    question,
immortality in the fantasy of being fed by the double
    mother,
of never being afraid of anyone—no academic deans, no
    Presidents great at fund-raising, no strict English
    Department Chairmen—

imagine being what hunger dreams it wants.
Everything's backwards in my mind.
The worker doesn't want to be boss, not much.
The boss doesn't love the girl curving in worship at his
    feet, not much.
I don't want oil deeds piled like shirts in my dresser, not
    much.
Work hard, don't get sick, do everything just right
or we'll put you away with the other crazies,
don't be different, don't be quite you, want, want, want,
lie back, bask in the unbroken warmth of money—
all this, forgive me, because a high school friend pocketed
    eight million bucks, I hear,
and won't be happy until he gets more, more.

One

You stood up in a dream
yelling at me not to envy
the plush chairs, silver, crystal
in a rich man's dining room,
smiling a little
as you reached to touch me.
Even after I shaved and ate
your echo came.
Since then my voice is colder, gruff,
I've noticed you don't smile
in snapshots, but withdraw
into the dead void of yourself
beyond, where no one is,
except in one: playing shuffleboard
on a cruise ship to Havana
in the late Thirties.
You sport wide flannel pants
that flare violently,
immaculate, bright white flags
faded by the shot's age.
Passengers line the deck,
asleep in slatted chairs
or amused by the game
and, as the puck (blurred inches from your stick)
takes off, you twist sideways,
facing the camera, grinning,
as if you knew I'd be here
to speak to you.
But it's the thick hardwood disc
that ended who knows where

your aim sent it I hear—
clacking the others apart,
nosing up to a bunch,
missing them all, sliding
across the court lines
in its lone silence.

In Washington Square

There's a man
who sits on a bench in the park nearby
and holds his arm across his eyes all day.
Sometimes he gets up and sits on the grass and stares down
as if he's pondering a hole
and would die if he turned away,
like someone who keeps checking himself in mirrors
to see if he exists.
He raises his arm to stay alive, he believes,
not against the sun, or me, or anything,
he's protecting the world from himself, and himself
from being gone, and God from seeing him.

Today, walking to work, I passed him in his frail, grisly
    clothes
and lifted my arm to sense
what it's like to be in pure fear.
Crickets ticked in the park. The fountain's thick, lusty
    plume
gushed and swayed, squirrels rode the branches.
On my way home there he was again, cross-legged on the
    grass,
head down, growling how God's not infinite, not perfect,
not everywhere, not beautiful, not, not, not,
and, like us, can't be known, and (who knows why)
an essay about fish that bite each other's mouths
before they copulate came to mind: the female
sticks her eggs on the side of a rock and the male
glides across, fertilizing them, then both
gulp mouthsful of sand and squirt it to slice trenches

the eggs will rest in. The white eggs
brocade the rock like a cloud of pearls
sewn on the bodice of a gown. Twilight—
a lullaby of cars and water,
the peace of illusion—
he began to rock, *dovening* the Jews call it, the death
    motion,
the fluctuating drone of the griever,
the darker it got the faster he rocked, back and forth back
    and forth,
the hypnotic frayed thread of his cry
coming from nowhere.

A Weather

God knows what really goes on between us,
God knows why I woke today seeing Marty's pimply face.
His dad's eyes, I hear, were taken out: cancer.
Adele, I hear, married a skin doctor and lived happily ever
    after,
I hear the little prick who played right field went to
    Dartmouth,
sold insurance then got some rare mouth tumor.
This is one of those days when everything's equal:
war, high school, famine, athlete's foot, asters, dog shit,
    everything
is a leaf on any tree any place you look,
and the words *beauty* and *truth*, twin sisters,
know exactly what each is thinking and feeling.
Thinking and *feeling*—what a miracle
to have two words that need each other to exist.
It's one of those chilly blue September days of pure energy
when from the moment you shave, shower, and dress
you feel so good you don't even remember who you are,
you hear the fat city trees chortling and shedding,
sweet voices in your head deciding to reach out
to readers you've never known, to a nation you'll never
    see,
to your friends, to a fistful of dust called Father, racking
this Fifties steel Underwood, green, festooned with
    chrome.

A God

Alone at night in my room,
typing these words,
baffled by what they will be
as evening blackens a patch of moss on a tree trunk,
chandeliers of brown seeds, stuttering birds,
I go back:
my daughters chat about school
or I'm reciting that great short poem *The Wind Shifts*,
catching pain in a student's eyes,
and I can't tell whose life is mine.
In yellow light a woman dusts a table
then sits reading for awhile.
In the alley a dog squats. Its master
hobbles out on crutches, stands by, watches,
and as I try these lines,
whispering to myself, to anyone, to you,
a pale shadow in a nightgown
appears in the kitchen doorway.
Light winks between her thighs
where the bare curves almost meet,
but her face, what she feels, what's between us
are invisible, unknown. Mother,
the tart, oily, blood-loud lipstick you wore
when I was thirteen, in bed, choked with asthma,
and you'd bend to kiss me . . .
I can taste its sour smear now. Last night,
with friends, I told them how I
picked my father's grave, paid for it,
bought the stone, had the ashes put in,
how you still won't go near any of it.

The man has dragged himself back in.
The woman, inside now, too,
leans over him trapped in his white waist-high cast
on the floor, legs propped on a fruit crate,
a miniature TV between his fat white feet:
moon-blue forms squirm over his face, over
the stove and pots, long spoons and glasses,
shift, seem to embody
those final meanings I still seek
in books about God.
She sets the table, puts out a steaming bowl,
near a jar with tall red flowers
spreading from it, she lights a candle.
The man's head follows her. Birds hunch on the branches,
    in the eaves,
and the truth that all I love, all I have touched
will die floods me. *Liar! Liar!*
I hear you, Mother, drunk, screaming on the phone last
    week.
Lamps, chairs,
each worn familiar object shines.
Wind jolts the branches.
The air halts like a sleeper's breath between our houses.
It's like being a god, seeing this.

Untitled Moon Poem

[July 20, 1969]

Predict? Tell yourself why? Nibble a cheese sandwich?
    Know?
The clouds keep moving but they can't say anything
and I am kissing my wife in the moonlight
for the tenthousandth time. Tears are beginning
    somewhere.
I see scuffed suitcases upstairs
bulging with memories and hopes and fun,
I imagine a nose-shaped country, and a ship
taking us to the shores of pale cold dust.
When the first man sinks onto the moon
I'm going to unravel *my* American flag
in the bathroom and plant it among towels and
    underpants,
I'm going to turn on the hot water and let the steam
hide me from galaxies, progress, and the poor
sweating their balls off across the street.
My head is riddled with pain.
The sky still has its huge cumuli.
My daughters get home from school, jabbering.
A popular muggy night in Philadelphia. And what?
Papers and the tube offering shots of the moon.
My life seems to have grown. But what?
Eat dinner? Answer the phone? Laugh? Cry?
That influential sphere is a sad balloon.
Its so-called female soul exhales sterile perfume
and a voice throbs out of it *Go on Go on.*

Slater

The police captain who lay in the room with my father
had had throat cancer, but the chemicals they used
sifted down, rotted his hip sockets.
The night before his operation to implant new ones
I was sitting between their beds, watching TV,
talking with my father about his few main themes:
death, sex, money; about his favorite line:
"It's a great life, if you don't weaken,"
weighing each man's silence.
Three doctors appeared. One said, "Mr. Slater, how do
    you feel?"
"Fine," he smiled. "You won't tomorrow," the surgeon
    intoned,
in what still sounds like a steel file drawer closing.
Slater came from a Pennsylvania coal town
where the mines, he told me, had shut down long ago—
a few bars with a jukebox and pool table in weak red light,
    grocery, garage,
cramped, dour, white wood-frame houses squeezed along
    one street.
Next afternoon after six hours on the table
he was back, writhing, somewhere else, not Slater.
Five days like that—no one, nowhere.
And yet Slater walked out on crutches after a slow
    recuperation,
smiling, as usual, grateful for having a life,
the fearlessness I had seen on my visits intact.
I wish I knew his secret—"attitude?" "training?" "guts?"
faith that "things will work out?"
Often I'd sit between them, the tube on, sound off,

trying to name it. He was big, in his late forties,
thick muscular forearms, warm grainy hands,
the creased, coarse face you get from too little sleep, too
    few amenities,
too much worry about others, a solid calm
rooted in listening.
His immediate kindness, his full unmediated smile,
an essence that seemed like saintly laughter
return sometimes when I'm low.
God knows what he knew.

Now and Then

A man who talks to the cold caves knows
what it is to hate himself, and not change, and feel
    nothing
deliberately, and sit, sit, sit until
a calm silences the heart, an unearthly, sick chill,
and nothing moves inside you, nothing
makes sense but a faint whistling
between car horns, doors, street words, dogs,
as if a teakettle somewhere on the block were boiling.
Tell yourself the story of a childhood
when nobody tired of life, nobody
woke up not wanting to play ball or go sledding
or even saluting the flag before classes
because it was great just being there—friends, naptime,
    recess—
not knowing the answers in Arithmetic,
instructed by some distant note buzzing on the windows.

Calling

Heavy rain batters the leaves,
brown branches.
A few birds keep calling,
one shakes itself out under the eaves
of the house next door,
ivy crawls over a rotting windowframe.
I call my mother.
"It won't be long now," she says,
the little bird alone,
huddling under the gutters of the roof,
its feathers drenched apart.
"It's like a flash,"
a seventy-five-year-old Japanese priest said today
on TV, "You touch an ancient cup and it returns your
        touch."
Vines finger the top of the window
just beneath the roof, where the sparrow
hides. Sky blinks through its tail feathers,
it takes off, comes back, shivers on a branch,
vanishes. "Surfaces may change but the core
like a long string is iron . . ."—the priest,
concluding his interview—.
We drift through our silences, we talk,
hearing no rain now,
letting each other know
we're still here.

After Talking about God

Yesterday a colleague told me his father died.
"Now there's just freedom," he said.
At the funeral, the tame, suspicious Jews
he grew up with hugged him, kissed him.
He'd mock them as a kid—their long black coats, their
    sidecurls.
Now he pinches the ragged clay face
of a bust that still doesn't have a nose, mouth, eyes.
He lets his beard grow.
His eyes cloud in the middle of a word.
He flips open a magazine to a shot of our galaxy—
light takes one hundred seventy-five thousand years
to cross it—its white swirls haunt the page
in the dust-infested studio.
I won't budge,
the mouth of the first girl I loved is hard, scared,
both our tongues inside me, I still taste
the deep blank kiss of Nothing.

Sketch

This place at the beginning of winter flares
until its last yellow is earth,
and you know what is not yours:
everything, even yourself,
trying to find words, or not.
You step to the window, inside and outside dark,
and lift it to the first brief chill
of far snow. Shapes lurch through the woods,
and their cries threaten as they go.
Dedicated to what there is
of naked vine and leaf, you wait
lost in the silence the word is.

Oblivion

1

I thought the Greek root would tell me something I didn't
    know
but there is no Greek root—ME, MF, fr. L. oblivion-,
    oblivio
and then to forget, perhaps fr. ob- *in the way* + *levis*
    smooth—
an act or instance of forgetting . . . but I thought it meant
    something like where we go
after death, i.e. "to oblivion," the future of us, the true,
inescapable condition of existence without consciousness,
human consciousness. So it's being forgotten more than
    anything
that hurts us, and immortality is—to be remembered?
What it really means is what someone said to me a few
    months ago
when I said "I've always thought of you as immortal, I
    guess,
but now I know you're not." "Yes, I am. I'm in your
    mind," he replied.
It's that "in your mind" that has a kind of murderous
    tenderness,
it's like saying someone *let* himself be part of you, to help
    you, yes,
but also because he trusted he could not be destroyed by
    your mind,
just as a mother takes up a screaming baby into her arms
and croons to it and pats it over and over Now Now Now
    she whispers and presses

the helplessly small body to her breast and it
calms, whimpers, calms fully and falls asleep there.

2

The elephant-gray elms bathed in overcast light glow.
Cobalt-blue sky peeps through hills of shaggy clouds.
Windy and cold, 30 on the thermometer outside my
     window,
chirpings off to my right from behind Jim Wilson's house,
branches stripped clean, bouncing and waving, the day
     bright, brighter,
then darkening under speeding clouds, everything held,
accepted, in an order, the mind and world one
forgetting in which only this moment has meaning. It's
     much much clearer now.
All's changed color: the lime-freckled salmon brick of Jim's
     house,
for example, suddenly flares crimson, fists of ailanthus
     pods
and stuccoed housewalls seem the same bleached tan,
     even the copper cross
(lived here ten years and I never noticed it) perched on the
     church tower
a block northeast is greener, complete because of the light.
But it's the jumble of stacked, rusting
tricycles and two-wheelers leaning against the side of a
     house on the backyard shed roof
and the oval yellow plastic wading pool tilted on edge

next to them and the cement bucket, white, left on
    the shed and, most, the homemade red
white and blue doghouse set down a few feet from the
    shed
that give this life its fullness, for now—
the innocent, peaked, green tarpaper roof and doorless
    door look kind,
a gift of absent hands, of animals taken in, fed.

From the Bridge

This time it happened as he crossed
the bridge over the defunct
railroad spur behind the warehouse—
Do it Do it—he counted
the rusted tracks, bouquets
of tall weed, fat concrete sockets
for the feet of the silver bridge.
Do it Do it Do it this time
it took that form. He stopped
and cautiously observed all
the things that had been cast there,
shoes, years of paper, bottles,
cans, boxes, car parts, weird shapes.
Which is what we become so why
worry or try to comprehend
anything even that impulse
tolling in his skull, that two-word
delicate command from some
source of revelation and grace
and truth at the core of his mind.
The mind does have a "core,"
where life and death are the same,
where nothing matters, not even
. . . who knows? The day was fairly clear
and not hot, "pleasant" is probably
the word you'd hear if you dialed
the weather, and yet there was nothing
he could do about
the desire of others. *Do it*
was the result of absorbing

that desire, he understood, as he
leaned on the scabby, dented rail,
a desire to have more, to
know what will come next, to
be sure of why and when.
But how can we *have* those?
"When nothing you do will do, what
do you do?" Hisamatsu asks,
and that's about the same as *Do it*,
in a voice not his, not anyone's,
the anonymous possibility
of choosing this. Well, he was walking to
his office, Saturday, to clear up
work, write letters, think,
he was trying to connect his pain
with something that would modify
his relationship to pain,
make it no particular person's,
certainly not his. But all he
knew was the unqualified
numb feeling on the bridge that
to be alive is not better
than to lie with the tracks, waste
metal, paper, and glass
like a thing, and why not, he thought, why not,
after all it *is* someone else,
not me, chanting that puny sentence
Do it Do it like the crowd
at a football game, and it must be
wonderful not to want at all

like junk decaying on cinders
that winks when you move your head.

Gratitude

Sunday. Nothing to do. I park.
Stumps, twigs, crates sail by, gusts wrinkle the water,
blur it, breath on a mirror.
The river's high, the soft banks barely hold it,
sun surfaces and sinks behind haze,
too early for the spectacular pink fire of the cherry,
and in me I hear again Jeff say
"My mother and her mother needed each other so much
they died three weeks apart," in me
my mother cries bitterly for the love she needs
and I'm like a child raging with useless love,
but I listen,
the suffering I brought with me almost gone.
I light a cigar and watch the wrapper blacken.
I think of my mother someday being gone,
of Jeff's father—when we met last, a month before he
 died,
we discussed the plump strawberries he raised each year
 on his apartment balcony,
the rows of boxes swelling with fruit,
how he loved their tart sweet taste.
One day the first people who loved you are gone—
"unparented helplessness" Brodkey calls it in a story
about himself as a kid listening to his mother
raging, incapable of love, crazy, dying of cancer,
begging for help, refusing to let him help.
It begins to rain. Driving back,

I scan the brown-green, wavy layers of creased urgent slate
    hillside
glistening five stories high, and Buson's thirteen rocks,
punctuating the infinite, appear,
Stryk's *Awakening*, at dusk
where he is taken into the darkness, joyfully, like the trees,
    "fully aware,"
Lu Yu's old old man running his hands delicately over
    rocks,
sighing, wondering, "Why can't I make myself stony, like
    you?"
appear and will always appear.
Wild, truculent geese pass over, honk, hang
on a shelf of wind until it breaks and they veer away.
It rains harder. The windshield blurs and clears.
On the other bank waves claw at steps built into the water,
trees shine, slow lines of cars,
dense, florescent red azaleas bush upon bush crowd the
    road—
each flower has a second one nesting inside—
the birds and rocks gone,
the people gone, the oldest human pain—
not being oneself wholly—gone.

In It

I love being here, like this.
Off to my right, the gold cross of a church,
dumb, tense, symmetrical, there;
soft, late afternoon, pink,
pre-spring Philadelphia light. Beautiful.
I'm in it now, seeing us on the way back
from teaching all day at the University.
March 12th, about 6 o'clock.
Stacks, buildings, wires, billboards, all on the sky,
all the horizon. Driving like this I hear—

inside the bubble of the car,
inside the pure, perceiving, thoughtlessly calm mind—
I know I know it it is there there
You sit next to me, listening,
staring ahead at nothing, everything.
I know that flower of emptiness
when the self touches the world in a deep blur
and the mind opens and is anything;
know, too, the plain, unintrospective sense

of being here: roofing is advertised,
rugs, Toyotas, office furniture; darkness
seeping in turns the sky a vague blood color,
each thing begins to be another,
and, for a time, being human is this.
Air *shhh*, tires *shhh*, the engine
taking us by warehouses, row houses, bleak
hulks and uninviting streets, off-ramps. Lights go on,

inaudibly, sky inky blue. Back there, we saw
grass stubbling the cold, mild fields of Princeton.

Back there, birds undulated in a flock,
black, ominous dots gathering—a shape, a flow—
like indecipherable words that were alive, true.
Now, as we descend the ramp,
I'm with my students in the classroom—they ask,
grimace, doze, read, study the walls, the sky;
empty of this time and place, I'm back—
I love being there with them, talking poetry, seized
        unexpectedly
by pine boughs caught in a high wind thrashing against
        the windows while Andy
Gratz explains in his casual, clinical way
something difficult in another's poem.

I could sit all day in that seedy room
just listening, butting in, trying to say why
rhythm and meaning *must* be one, etc.
We glide under the immense, blue, concrete-and-steel
footings of the Walt Whitman Bridge, and feel small.
Black and white wavy bars, like the hide of a zebra,
stamp the blacktop. Light through a grating. Here.
Light fuzzy with smoke and time as it grows dark. Back
        there.
Driving with you asleep, I see
eye-level red clouds scooting across; raw

seeded hills, scallop-topped, sprouting in patches, washed
	pale brown, green, following both sides of the road.
And distance, hazeless after yesterday's hard rain.
I'm in it, as I just said,
and what it is is who I am, and then
the phrase *is there* stuns me and won't go away.
I dip my hand into a half-pound bag
of peanuts I bought with Bob at a store across
from the Writing Program office. We were talking about
	poetry.
He bought Camels, and said maybe
we'd see each other again soon, maybe
in Philly, where I am now, as

I zip past the bridge and turn right for home,
down Second Street: brooms, ladders, mattresses, stoves
	spotlighted in windows.
He wore an old tan corduroy shirt, sweater, dungarees.
Two different thickness laces in scuffed shoes.
Reg, Ted, Michael, Bob and I
sat in my office discussing prosody.
I grab three or four nuts and crack one
with one hand and steer the wheel with the other, flick off
half the shell and pop two into my mouth and chew.

In the store Bob and I discussed prose, too,
whose truth is desire satisfied immediately
when no meaning lurks behind or deep in it.
Is there anything we can say we know?

It's near dark now; we reach the block-long Greek Revival
    Free Library.
Starlings by the thousands vibrate, as always, below
its grim, official cornices; their lewd,
meaningless twitterings could be a sign. Lawn lights bathe

the facade, and it reminds me when I was a kid I'd switch
    on a flashlight
under my chin at Halloween to look ugly, scary.
Wide-eyed I'd rehearse in dark in the bathroom mirror.
Small pleasures now; being at one with you.
I think I know where I am, and who; and turn right.
Up the hill. Know. Don't know. Neither. At a lecture last
    night
the speaker told an anecdote about a poet-friend of his
who felt sure that the woman in a certain Vermeer had
    finished licking her lips just
before the expression she has in the painting. Because of
    the moisture
you can see glistening—now; because of the strangely
    unfinished closure.

And, hearing that, something joyful about time came
    clear—
because we want to be so alive, because
we're afraid to be here. Brief, human touches become
    everything:
light on an eyelid; clean, blond hair; half-consciously
    whistling an old popular tune;

words needed, words received; a warm look—
as I park and scoop up my briefcase and raincoat,
slide out, lock the car, step into my house.
One light dissolves into another,
this 10 × 10 kind of song
talking, making itself free of my tongue.

Poetry from Illinois

History Is Your Own Heartbeat
Michael S. Harper (1971)

The Foreclosure
Richard Emil Braun (1972)

The Scrawny Sonnets and
Other Narratives
Robert Bagg (1973)

The Creation Frame
Phyllis Thompson (1973)

To All Appearances: Poems New
and Selected
Josephine Miles (1974)

Nightmare Begins Responsibility
Michael S. Harper (1975)

The Black Hawk Songs
Michael Borich (1975)

The Wichita Poems
Michael Van Walleghen (1975)

Cumberland Station
Dave Smith (1977)

Tracking
Virginia R. Terris (1977)

Poems of the Two Worlds
Frederick Morgan (1977)

Images of Kin: New and
Selected Poems
Michael S. Harper (1977)

On Earth as It Is
Dan Masterson (1978)

Riversongs
Michael Anania (1978)

Goshawk, Antelope
Dave Smith (1979)

Death Mother and Other Poems
Frederick Morgan (1979)

Local Men
James Whitehead (1979)

Coming to Terms
Josephine Miles (1979)

Searching the Drowned Man
Sydney Lea (1980)

With Akhmatova at the Black Gates
Stephen Berg (1981)

More Trouble with the Obvious
Michael Van Walleghen (1981)

Dream Flights
Dave Smith (1981)

The American Book of the Dead
Jim Barnes (1982)

Northbook
Frederick Morgan (1982)

The Floating Candles
Sydney Lea (1982)

Collected Poems, 1930–83
Josephine Miles (1983)

The River Painter
Emily Grosholz (1984)

The Passion of the
Right-Angled Man
T. R. Hummer (1984)

Healing Song for the Inner Ear
Michael S. Harper (1984)

Dear John, Dear Coltrane
Michael S. Harper (1985)

Poems from the Sangamon
John Knoepfle (1985)

Eroding Witness
Nathaniel Mackey (1985)
National Poetry Series

The Ghosts of Who We Were
Phyllis Thompson (1986)

In It
Stephen Berg (1986)